Woman Preach

By Rev. Dr. Louis Blake Hathorn

_____
Signature

_____
Date

Blog: meredithetc.com
facebook Meredith *Etc*
🐦 Meredith*etc*

Visit the Author's Book Page to make comments
http://meredithetc.com/woman-preach/

A Meredith *Etc* Book

Meredith *Etc*
1052 Maria Court
Jackson, Mississippi 39204-5151
www.meredithetc.com

All rights reserved. No part of this book may be reproduced in any form or by any means, electronic or mechanical including photocopying, recording or by any information storage without written permission from the Publisher.

Published simultaneously by Meredith *Etc* in softcover/hardback
Trade paperback 6"x 9" printed by CreateSpace (Amazon)
Hardback edition 6"x 9" printed by Nook Press (Barnes & Noble)

Woman Preach © June 2017 Rev. Dr. Louis Blake Hathorn
Thesis © 2012 *Women Struggling from the Pew to the Pulpit*

Meredith Coleman McGee, Foreword
Kay Higginbotham, Introduction

Keywords: Phoebe Palmer, women's rights, famous women, Sojourner Truth, women preachers

First Printing
Trade Paperback Edition 6"x 9" -- 87 pages
Black & White on White paper
ISBN-13: 978-0692718209
ISBN-10: 0692718206
Available on the World Wide Web as an eBook
Library of Congress Prints & Photographs Div. Washington, D.C.
Cover - Famous Aviatrix Ruth Nichols

Visit Rev. Dr. Louis Blake Hathorn's author page online.
https://meredithetc.com/woman-preach/

> *A book is a gift you can open again and again.*
> —*Garrison Keillor*

THIS BOOK IS A GIFT TO:

_____

FROM: _____

DATE: _____

TABLE OF CONTENTS

FOREWORD	vii
INTRODUCTION	xi

CHAPTERS

1	*Women in Ministry: An Historical Analysis*	2
2	*Famous Female Preachers/Feminists: 1800 – 1970*	26
3	*Modern Women Stand in the Pulpit*	41
4	*Popular Women Preachers*	49
5	*The Future of Women in Ministry*	56
	CONCLUSION	59
	BIBLIOGRAPHY	62
	ABOUT THE AUTHOR	67
	DEDICATION	68
	ACKNOWLEDGEMENTS	69
	NOTES	71

ADVANCE PRAISE for *Woman Preach*

In this recent book, *Woman Preach*, The Reverend Dr. Louis Blake Hathorn, sheds new light on the powerful role women played in the church, and in society. From Sojourner Truth to Susan B. Anthony, both 19th century preachers, women have been a source of strength, acting with the prophetic voices of social justice, to abolish slavery and bigotry and to treat women and all people with equality and the dignity they deserve.

Dr. Hathorn provides insight into the, often muted and misrepresented, leadership roles women played in the church, articulating the needs of the poor and the neglected. History shows, documented in Dr. Hathorn's book, that it was the women of the church who called upon its leadership to answer the challenge of the Gospel in addressing those needs. *Woman Preach* deserves to be studied for its timeless truths.

◊ Reverend G. David Singleton, *Minister, Social Justice Activist, Humanitarian.* NOTE: Rev. Singleton wrote the foreword for Rev. Hathorn's first book *Social Justice and Christianity*.

From the onset, one can tell *Woman Preach* is a labor of love left to the world by Rev. Dr. Louis B. Hathorn. His passion for his subject matter pours out on each page, and the depth of his research is impressive.

◊ Vanessa M. Cavett, *Author*

Overcoming Church Conflict: Confessions of a Church Girl, and *Act like a Woman of God: A Christian Woman's Guide to Men, Relationships and Godly Character*

FOREWORD

Bishop Willie J. Coleman, a friend of my famous uncle James Howard Meredith, referred Rev. Louis Blake Hathorn to our typing and editorial service in 2011. When Rev. Hathorn walked in our living room to discuss getting his thesis typed and edited, I had no idea we would one day convert it into a book, or that I was gaining a friend, or that this small-town preacher had so much knowledge to share with the world.

Five years ago, *Woman Preach* was Rev. Hathorn's thesis, *Women Struggling From the Pews to the Pulpit* which he presented in seminary as partial credit toward his Masters degree in Theology. Turns out, this really is a small world because his wife, Claranett, and I have common ancestors by way of Attala County, Mississippi; the day after he graduated in 2012 she called me and said with pride, "Louis was salutatorian of his class."

His school status confirmed that he had penned a great work. Rev. Hathorn continued his studies, and started working on his dissertation, a study of Christian social justice leaders. Historic pictures added new life to spiral bound academic documents on bond paper that usually occupy a school library shelf serving merely as a model paper to incoming students.

His dissertation was renamed *Social Justice and Christianity*; it was converted into a textbook. It was released in August of 2015. His book release party broke the Friends of the Lexington Public Library's crowd record.

Rev. Hathorn was enthusiastic about completing *Woman Preach*. He told me on several occasions, "Everybody keeps asking about the book. I told them, it's coming soon," then he smiled. By the Summer of 2016, he had a proof copy in his hand and was looking for someone to write the Introduction. We planned to release the book by the end of the year. None of that happened; he became critically ill, and never recovered. At his funeral in Noxapater, Mississippi, my family, and I sat in folded chairs in the church entrance. Dozens of men lined the walls in front of the building because the church had reached full capacity. His popularly shed light on a life well lived.

After I suffered through my pain, I realized Rev. Hathorn will have that familiar, triumphant smile on his face when *Woman Preach* reaches the market. Our publishing company, Meredith Etc, acquired two significant historical works when we signed contracts to publish his master thesis and dissertation. I am honored to help bring his second book forth.

Like most southern Black Baptist preachers, for years, Rev. Hathorn told me he felt the pulpit was reserved for men. He said the idea that women can preach just stung him like a bee, like the swift passing of a wintery breeze. The book was named "Woman Preach" because God revealed to Rev. Hathorn that He gives women the power to preach the gospel to lost souls.

Frankly, in some ways, *Woman Preach*, reflects our imperfect society. One hundred and fifty years ago, women could not vote, and few could own property. Whole Indian tribes were displaced, African freedmen were second class citizens, immigrants were welcomed by the thousands, our country was governed by White males, and horses and horse drawn wagons were the usual mode of transportation. European immigrants gathered the loot from wars. The haves were few; yet, have nots were plentiful; immigrants in pursuit of happiness, desiring a slice of the spoils, united and challenged their young government. Limited equality standards emerged, but life continued and the country came into its own.

The right of citizens to peacefully assemble is a fundamental part of our government. However, a platform for women to speak their minds was hidden for centuries because the thought of a woman speaking behind a podium was socially intolerable. Scholarly literature portrayed women as weak, needy, and childlike beings. The brainwashing was so morbid; it could not be cut with a knife. Women had to knock down brick walls held together by men to walk through doors, but a determined few marched onward in search of equality.

As Hathorn noted, "In 1838, a public address by a woman in Philadelphia sparked a riot. When the rioters calmed down the meeting hall had been destroyed (36)."

Woman Preach is a very revealing, scholarly work. Four things struck me the most:

1. The story of how Sojourner Truth, an illiterate former African woman, transferred herself from a runaway slave to an evangelist and social reformer,
2. The childlike status of women in Colonial America,
3. The fact that 19th century preachers were more powerful than the printing press, and
4. The revelation that the 1848 Women's Rights Conference was built upon a coalition of Quakers, abolitionists, preachers, and statesmen.

Before the Civil War, Republicans - the party of Abraham Lincoln - raised their voices against the inhumane system of chattel slavery. After the war, the party lifted their voices in favor of the social, economic, and political advancement of freedmen. Republicans, of years long gone, led a populous movement for moral issues which was strategically opposed by its southern economic benefactors.

Nearly 150 years after the Civil War, two women on the opposite ends of national politics broke the glass ceiling during the 2016 presidential campaign. Kellyanne Conway, became the first woman to manage a presidential campaign for the Republican Party. She was sworn in, January 21, 2017, as the Counselor to the President. Secretary of State, Hillary Clinton, the first woman to lead the presidential ticket of a major political party, became the first female presidential candidate to win the popular vote: 65,844,954. She lost the election to Business Tycoon, Donald John Trump, who obtained 62,979,879 general votes, but won the electoral college – 306 v. her 232 votes. Only two other presidential candidates, both Republicans, previously won their presidential bids via the electoral college: Benjamin Harrison (1889-93); and George Walker Bush (2001-09).

Millions of voters view the Electoral College as a severe flaw in a democratic system. Saturday, January 21, 2017, the day after the inauguration of Pres. Donald Trump, one million women around the world led solidarity marches in opposition to the political ideology of Pres. Trump and the Republican party. Women publicly objected to Pres. Trump's stance against abortion, his call to build a wall between Mexico and the U.S.A., his promise to implement a Muslim ban, and his effort to repeal the Affordable Care Act. Women and their allies also opposed Pres. Trump's racy cabinet picks, and the U.S. intelligence report that Russian computer hackers altered the 2016 presidential campaign.

Throughout history, men have violently protected cultural norms. Today, the U.S.A. is as polarized as it was in the 19th century when the Civil War was dawning. Abolitionists Lloyd William Garrison and Frederick Douglass supported the Women's Rights Movement in 1848. Like Douglas and others, Congressman John Lewis stood with women, during the Women's Marches, January 21, 2017. During "Bloody Sunday" John Lewis, a former 1961 Freedom Rider, and the former chairman of the Student Non-Violent Coordinating Committee, marched for voting rights with Martin Luther King Jr. in 1965. John Lewis was severely beaten and other protestors were stomped by the hooves of horses, several died.

Freedoms have never been free. Surely, the laws are not always just. Women have come a long way; but, for many, the struggle for full inclusion in society continues.

By Meredith Coleman McGee,
Author, Publisher, Lecturer, Business Entrepreneur
www.typingsolutions.biz ★ www.meredithetc.com

INTRODUCTION

I am delighted to read Dr. Louis Blake Hathorn's book, *Woman Preach*, giving credence to women preachers. There have always been "women preachers" and they have filled a mighty place in history as evidenced here in this work. They were correct to lead whether or not they were approved, accredited or otherwise legitimized by the powers that existed in the community structure at the time and place they existed. God needed them, God called them, and God used them! And He is doing so today, in this place.

Women can preach...... pray...... administer...... heal...... counsel...... comfort...... lead worship...... serve...... write ...... lead people to Jesus ...... inspire...... love...... bring justice...... give hope and joy...... witness...... teach...... mediate...... or meditate. Whatever it is that God requires, a woman is able.

This book gives many beautiful examples of women and how they have served God, the church, and the people. Let this book serve as an inspiration to those who feel the call that their services are needed. The world has many wrongs to be righted. To deny the talents of over half its population is a grave injustice to all.

I felt the call early in my life to be a missionary. My favorite place to talk to God was sitting in a pine tree in the middle of a huge field with wind softly whistling through it. It was between God and me alone in the pine tree. Not those who devise organizational structures. Not those who aren't accepting of a woman's call to preach. Certainly, obstacles can get in the way. It's not an easy way, but if a woman is called, it's THE way.

There is a part of the marriage ceremony that states emphatically: "What God has joined together, let no man put asunder." I would paraphrase that to say, "Whomever God has called to Himself and to His service, let no man put asunder."

Women Can Preach! Woman Preach!!

Kay Higginbotham, Contributing Author
Virtues from the Heart

REV. DR. LOUIS BLAKE HATHORN STANDING
LEXINGTON PUBLIC LIBRARY
LEXINGTON, MISSISSIPPI

Woman Preach

ONE

Women in Ministry: An Historical Analysis

"The word 'gospel' is the English translation of the Greek word, *eu-anggellion* which means 'beautiful message' or 'good news.'"[i]

Unlike factual news, 'good news' is soul-saving news, mind liberating news, burden-lifting, heart-fixing, fellowship creating, people empowering, joy-inspiring, earth-redeeming, world-reconciling, and problem-solving news.[ii] Ella Pearson Mitchell argued against blocking someone from delivering the 'good news' because God owns His own news agency. The 'good news' does not require one to believe in the messenger, but to accept the message. It does not matter whether the messenger is African, Arab, male or female, he or she has been sent to proclaim God's message.

An historical overview of the bible and early Christianity has shown that although men were predominantly chosen to help spread the 'good news,' God definitely used women. "Women have been and are called by God to preach."[iii] The order established at creation gave men and women the same equality. The woman is bone of his bone and flesh of his flesh. Man is asked to leave his parents and cleave to his wife, and the couple are to be one, making them equal rather than hierarchical. In the third chapter of Genesis, Eve broke God's rule first and tempted Adam to be disobedient. For her sin, Eve and women are subjected to pain during childbirth and women became subordinates to their husbands. Many interpret this section conclusively because it clearly gives men rank over women.

During the Mosaic period, Miriam was a prophetess. She led the people in songs and she also taught them the law. The book of Micah acknowledged that the Israelites were given Moses, Aaron, and Miriam to lead them into the land of Egypt (Micah 6:4). The next woman in the Old Testament who had a significant leadership role was Deborah. She was a military leader and a judge. In Judges, Deborah was called a spiritual leader and a prophetess. In addition, she was a counselor, the governor-judge, and the leader of the triumphant army (Judges 4:4).

Rabbinical accounts of Deborah reported that she rose from the lamp keeper in the tabernacle to a counselor, judge, and seer. Deborah's role was so significant to Barak, General of the Army, until he would not go into battle against Sisera without Deborah at his side.

During the reign of King Josiah, the Israelites stopped worshiping in the temple which was in ruins. When the High Priest Hilkiah went through the debris and found some scrolls containing the law, he was not sure if all of them were authentic; therefore, King Josiah turned to a woman named Huldah for counsel. Huldah, a teacher and spiritual leader, was the wife of Shallum, who was the keeper of the king's wardrobe. Huldah evaluated the documents, warned the people of God's wrath against their idolatry, and they took her seriously.

Jesus showed great regard for women. He went against Jewish tradition to give reverence to women and others from other ethnic groups. For instance, Jesus had a conversation with a Samaritan woman at the well even though Jews abhorred Samaritans. In John 8:1-30, John noted that Jesus considered it unfair to stone the woman for adultery and not the man. During the upper room prayer, women, including Mary, were present. In Acts 2:17 women were filled with the spirit and prophesized. In addition, when the church expanded to homes, women were active, and they were not just hostesses.

Some ancient societies regarded women as inferior to men. The status of women in the society reshaped their authority as religious leaders. However, Jesus did not teach his disciples to embrace a hierarchy. He did not share ideas that gave the notion that one would be subordinate to another. For, He said to His disciples:

> Ye know that the princess of the Gentiles exercise dominion over them, and they that are great exercise authority upon them. But it shall not be so among you: but whosoever will be great among you, let him be your minister; and whosoever be chief among you, let him be your servant Matthew 20:25-27.

During the fourth century after the death of Christ, women studied the scriptures in the original languages and wrote inquisitive letters to male scholars seeking their insight on the written word. Faltonia Betitia Proba wrote a poem on the creation of the world and the life of Jesus Christ in Virgilian verse, and, female mystics recorded their visionary accounts to instruct their communities.

Historically, women played vital roles in religious ceremonial events, but based on various interpretations of scripture, and societal views of women, for centuries they were restricted primarily to subservient ministerial roles such as ushers, Sunday school teachers, and youth group leaders. In essence, for the past 300 years, women have been struggling to get from the pew into the pulpit. There are two major questions concerning this controversial issue:

1. Does the scripture authorize women to be preachers?
2. What societal norms rendered women subordinate and unequal?

Thousands of years ago, women played major roles in spiritual affairs. Miriam, the sister of Moses, was a prophetess and a member of the teaching team when Moses was leading the Israelites out of Egypt. Deborah was a counselor, governor-judge, and the leader of the triumphant army. Patriotic biases and prejudices based on sexism have been ruling principles throughout the ages.

As centuries passed, the role of women in society changed. The religious roles of women were restructured, as their societal positions were altered. During Jesus' life, women were stoned for adultery, while their male lovers were spared, Jews excluded non-Jews, women were dominated by males, and powerful groups enslaved weaker rivals.

As the least of citizens, women struggled for centuries to obtain equal rights. In 1848, The Women's Rights Movement was launched on American soil. These women collaborated with Quakers, anti-slavery advocates, former slaves, and others who used their collective voices to tell their countrymen they would not be quiet until equality was a priority of men who ruled the White house, congress, and preached from the pulpit. The activists lifted their voices to the heavens in song, with prayers, basing their beliefs on the word of God. Amen!

Some women walked, trotted, and travelled thousands of miles spreading the 'good news' to anyone who was willing to listen. Despite criticism, women continued to share God's love through their life, words, and deeds. Today, many churches have given up that old argument that women cannot teach nor have authority over men, and they are ordaining women and allowing them to be used by God as He sees fit.

Women used their voices to dispute the ideas that they were intellectually inferior. When African freedmen obtained the right to vote in 1870, women argued that they deserved the voting rights too. African American women were not primary or secondary in the Woman's Movement in the 20th century, but the movement had a universal effect. For instance, equal pay for equal work was universally desired.

A comprehensive list of the scripture relating to women's marital, family, and church roles are listed below in order to analyze the controversy surrounding the premise that the word of God gives women permission to teach women and children, but not to teach men.

Scripture Chart for Women in the Church

Citation	Scripture	Topic
1 Timothy 2:9-10	In like manner also, that women adorn themselves in modest apparel, with shamefacedness and sobriety; not with broided hair, or gold, or pearls, or costly array; but (which becometh women professing godliness) with good works.	How women should dress
Titus 2:3-5	That the aged women likewise, that they be in behavior as becometh holiness, not false accusers, not given to much wine, teachers of good things; that they may teach the	What women should teach by example

	young women to be sober, to love their husbands, to love their children	
1 Peter 3:1-6	Likewise, ye wives, be in subjection to your own husbands; that if any obey not the word, they also may without the word be won by the conversation of the wives; while they behold your chaste conversation coupled with fear. Whose adorning let it not be that outward adorning of plaiting the hair, and of wearing of gold, or putting on apparel; but let it be hidden man of the heart, in that which is not corruptible, even the ornament of a meek and quiet spirit, which is in the sight of God of great price. For after this manner in the old time the holy women also, who trusted in God, adorned themselves, being in subjection unto their own husbands: Even as Sara obeyed Abraham calling him lord: whose daughters ye are, as long as ye do well, and are not afraid with any amazement.	The subjugation of women.
1 Timothy 2:12	But I suffer not a woman to teach, nor to usurp authority over the man, but to be in silence.	Women cannot teach men
1 Corinthians 14:34-35	Let your women keep silence in the churches: for it is not permitted unto them to speak; but they are commanded to be under obedience, as also saith the law. And if they will learn anything, let them ask their husbands at home: for it is a shame for women to speak in the church.	Woman are required to let their husbands speak for them in church
1 Timothy 3:2, 12	A bishop then must be blameless, the husband of one wife, vigilant, of	Guidelines for bishops

	good behavior, given to hospitality, apt to teach. Let no man despise thy youth; but be thou an example of the believers, in spirit, in faith, in purity.	and deacons
Genesis 2:18, 23	And the Lord God said, It is not good that the man should be alone; I will make him a help mate for him. And Adam said, This is now bone of my bone, and flesh of my flesh: she shall be called Woman, because she was taken from Man.	Women were created to help men
Joel 2:28	And it shall come to pass afterward, that I will pour out my spirit upon all flesh; and your sons and your daughters shall prophesy, your old men shall dream dreams, your young men shall see visions.	Scripture regarding men and women prophets in the Old Testament
Acts 2:17	And it shall come to pass in the last days, saith God, I will pour out of my Spirit upon all flesh: and your sons and your daughters shall prophesy, and your men shall see visions, and your old men shall dream dreams.	Scripture regarding men and woman prophets in the New Testament
Acts 21:8-9	And the next day we that were of Paul's company departed, and came unto Caesarea and we entered into the house of Philip the evangelist, which was one of the seven; and abode with him. And the same man had four daughters, virgins, which did prophesy.	Early Christian female prophets (four daughters of Philip)
1 Timothy 2:11	Let the women learn in silence with all subjection.	Women learning silently.

Hebrews 6:10	For God is not unrighteous to forget your work and labour of love, which ye have shewed toward his name, in that ye have ministered to the saints, and do minister.	Christian ministry to each other
Romans 16:1	I command unto you Phebe our sister, which is a servant of the church which is at Cenchrea.	Phebe was a church servant
Ephesians 4:16	From whom the whole body fitly joined together and compacted by that which every joint supplieth, according to the effectual working in the measure of every part, maketh increase of the body unto the edifying of itself in love.	Christian fellowship and ministry
Galatians 3:28	There is neither Jew nor Greek, there if neither bond nor free, there is neither male nor female: for ye are all one in Christ Jesus.	Christian equality in terms of race and gender
1 Corinthians 11:8-9	For the man is not of the woman; but the woman of the man, neither was the man created for the woman; but the woman was created for the man.	The woman was created for the man.

The above scriptures fed the controversy which excludes women from becoming preachers and church leaders. Even today, there are widespread beliefs against women clergy. However, many believers have become mindful, female clergy such as Rev. Anne Graham Lotz and Rev. Barbara Brown Taylor are the exception rather than the norm.

Even though Lotz, Taylor, and other female preachers have carved a bigger piece of the preacher arena from their male nay sayers than their predecessors, they stand on the shoulders of Abigail Smith Adams, Mary Wollstonecraft, Sojourner Truth, and Amanda Berry Smith. Today, Lotz preaches to thousands in packed arenas, while Taylor has been dubbed one of the most effective preachers in the English-speaking world.

Mary Wollstonecraft, 1759 to 1797, 18th century feminist
Courtesy of the Library of Congress

Although, women struggled for centuries to be equal in the eyes of their male brothers of the cloth, much has changed in recent times. Surely, for some men, they will have to feel God's power at work through women to realize that God calls women to do His work, just like He calls men.

Historically, several women penned very important Christian works. A German abbess, Hildegard of Bingen (1098-1179), wrote three major theological treatises on creation, sin, salvation, and many other works. She was one of the first well known poets and prophetesses in Germany. Julian of Norwich (1342-1416), published her religious visions in 1395. It was the first known book in the English language to have been written by a woman. She described God as having paternal and maternal aspects. She said, "As truly as God is our father, so truly God is our mother."[iv]

The current debate over the role of women in Western society can be traced to activists such as Abigail Smith Adams, Mary Wollstonecraft, Emma Hart Willard, Sojourner Truth, Mary Lyon, and Catherine Beecher. First Lady Abigail Adams wrote to her husband in the White House that women would refuse to be bound by laws and a constitution that would be created without their input. Mrs. Adams view was like a soft whisper in the wind because she lived in a male dominated society.

During the 19th century, Emma Willard started a seminary for women. Afterward, women were elevated to a similar professional equivalence with men. However, throughout that period, women struggled to obtain rights in America and abroad. The U.S. Women's Rights Movement was organized in 1848, but it was not until 1920 that women obtained the right to vote.

According to Feminist Theologian Rosemary R. Ruether, excluding women from teaching the Word of God violates the redemptive vision of the gospels. Women concluded that the scripture in Timothy 2:13-14 said, "I permit no woman to

First Lady Abigail Smith Adams 1744-1818
Photo Courtesy of the Library of Congress
Wife of John Adams, 2nd US President 1797-1801
Women's Rights Advocate

teach or have authority over men, she is to keep silence," expressed one side of an argument; however, others of that era accepted women's leadership. Jesus himself accepted the full humanity of all people regardless of their gender or their status in society.

Emma Willard Seminary, Photo by Detroit Publishing Co. 1903

Paul praised Priscilla and her husband, whom he called fellow workers in Christ Jesus. The term 'fellow workers in Christ Jesus' referred to other leaders of the gospel ministry. Priscilla and her husband tutored Apollos, who was a preacher in the early Christian church. In his discussion of them, Paul used Priscilla's name first when he announced that the couple was a part of the teaching team indicating that Priscilla and not her husband was the primary teacher which contradicts scripture in the Gospel of Timothy condemning woman preachers.

Historical Chart of Women in the Church and in Catholicism

Period	Highlight
1st Century 1–100 AD	Mary Magdalene is a loyal follower of Jesus and prominent in his ministry. Jesus intervenes on her

	behalf in an argument she has with Peter, according to the Gospel of Thomas.
1st Century 1–100 AD	Several women – the deacon Phoebe, "fellow worker" Prisca, "workers in the Lord" Tryphena and Tryphosa, and 'apostal' Junia are among those Paul refers to in his letter to the Romans. Princess Aethelthryth founds her own monastery and becomes its abbess. Noble women in medieval times could often gain educational parity with men by becoming nuns.
12th Century 1101-1200 AD	Female mystic Hildegard of Bingen, abbess of Rupertsberg, is a well-known speaker and scholarly writer. The first universities in Europe were forming, but were all male.
1290s	Agnes Blannbekin is a mystic whose symbolic visions include naked nuns and priests dancing in heaven and herself swallowing the foreskin of Christ. Her visions were published amidst controversy in the 18th century.
14th Century 1301-1400 AD	Bridget of Sweden founded a respected monastic order and ultimately became one of the very few women canonized between 1300 and 1500. Her canonization was so contentious, however, that it had to be repeated three times.
1612	Spanish mystic, Teresa of Avila, of the Carmelite order, became a saint. King Philip III convinced the pope to make her co-patron of Spain in 1618, amid plenty of opposition.
1935	A commission appointed by the Archbishop of Canterbury and York found, "no compelling theological reasons for or against women," but insisted on maintaining the male priesthood.
1968	Pope Paul VI issued Humanea Vitae (Of Human Life) reaffirmed the Vatican's prohibition of all artificial forms of birth control, no matter how compelling the circumstance.
1976	A formal declaration from the pope praised women for all they have to offer, affirming that the Catholic Church "has never felt that priestly or Episcopal ordination can be conferred on women."
1988	Pope John Paul II affirmed the equality of women and men in his apostolic letter Muliens Dignitatem, noting the essential role women have played throughout Christian history and their value to the church.

	1989	First female bishops ordained by the Anglican Church of New Zealand and the Episcopal Church in the United States.
	1994	Ordination of women in the C of E began.
	2000	Report revealed nearly half of all male clergy refused to take communion from women priests.
	2003	The Scottish Episcopal Church allowed female bishops.
	2006	The first woman was elected to archbishop status in the Episcopal Church in the U.S.
endnotes		[v] [vi]

In a *New York Times* article, Neela Banerjee noted that while the Gospel of Timothy admonished women to be silent, St. Paul said in Galatians 3:28, "There is neither male nor female; for you are all one in Christ Jesus."[vii]

Salvation Army Founder William D. Booth argued that the fact that Jesus chose 12 men to be his disciples should not be interpreted that He did not intend for women to preach, and it was not confirmation against women preaching in the pulpit.

Other Christians contended this argument was weak and distorted because all 12 disciples were Jewish, and Christianity is open to all nationalities. Booth also pointed out that Jesus was indifferent to gender because He said, "Whoever does the will of God is my brother and my sister and mother" (Matthew 12:50).

In 1771, renown Methodist Preacher John Wesley was introduced to Mary Bosanquet, Sarah Crosby, and Sarah Ryan. Bosanquet ran an orphanage, and all three women preached the gospel; most women preachers attracted small audiences, but Crosby spoke to gatherings in the hundreds. Even though the women carried out God's mission to save souls, John Wesley discredited their soul saving work by referring to their preaching events as "class meetings."

William D. Booth, Salvation Army Founder, 1829-1912
Photo Courtesy of the Library of Congress
Methodist Preacher – Women's Rights Advocate
"The Prophet of the Poor."

Although women preached the 'good news' to lost souls, they were criticized because some suggested the scripture said women should not teach or have authority over men.

Bosanquet fired back by saying the scripture might mean, "Women should not take authority over their husband" (1 Timothy 2:12). She contended the scripture did not prevent women from entreating sinners to come to Jesus, to sharing their spiritual testimony, or from exercising their prophetic call to the ministry.

However, in June of 1771, Wesley reevaluated his bias against women preachers. He described Bosanquet's call to preach as an "extraordinary call." From that time onward, Wesley endorsed Crosby as a lay preacher. Historians consider John Wesley the founder of the women's Methodist preaching movement. Once he accepted the fact that God calls women to preach, he encouraged their actions. After his death, his successors discouraged and prohibited women once again from preaching and speaking in public.

A decade later, Bosanquet married Wesley's successor, John Fletcher. In 1803, a resolution was passed at the Methodist Conference banning women preachers. Despite the Methodist opposition to women preachers, Bosanquet preached five sermons a week until she died in 1815.

The Society of Friends was one of the first communities to endorse and encourage the public ministry of women. In their community, neither men nor women were ordained. During the 17th century, Quaker women were the first women to preach in England and also in the American colonies.

Smith, Bosanquet, Crosby, and Ryan were among the first Methodist women preachers in Great Britain. Wesley ordained the first Methodist preachers at the Methodist Episcopal Church in 1784. Barbara Heck, an early Irish Methodist colonist acquired the title *Foundress of American Methodism*. Heck once found a group of Irish Immigrants playing cards, and swept the cards in a fire. She believed God's message needed to spread. She encouraged her cousin, Philip Embury, to continue the lay preaching in America he had done in England. Philip complied and started preaching from his home and brought Methodism to New York.[viii]

Maggie Newton Van Cott was the first female minister ordained by the Methodist Episcopal Church. Cott was a travelling evangelist. By age 50, she had travelled 143,417 miles and preached nearly 10,000 revival meetings. A critic of Cott protested that her license didn't allow her to preach. She retorted that she had received her commission from God.

By the 18th century, the Methodist class movement gave rise to a larger group of women preachers who travelled in England preaching and teaching the word of God. Unlike the Methodist movement in England, women preachers were rare in the American colonies. So, when Phoebe Palmer began to speak publicly, she became a novelty. Palmer and her sister administered a "Tuesday Meeting for the Promotion of Holiness," for over 30 years.[ix] The popularity of the meeting helped launch Palmer's successful public speaking career.

During the 1840s, she took her meeting to another level and began to lead revivals in the United States and Canada. From 1859 to 1863, Phoebe and her husband Walter led revivals throughout the British Isles. Neither of them were ordained and they did not have to abide by church rules and were able to go wherever they were invited. Phoebe published a widely read monthly journal, wrote seven books, advocated for women's right to speak, and spoke to large crowds in the United States, Canada, and Britain.

Amanda Berry Smith was a notable woman preacher of African descent in the 1800s. She was an African Methodist

Episcopal Minister. Bishop. J.M. Thoburn remarked of Smith, "I felt in a second she was possessed of a rare degree of spiritual power."[x] According to Tate, Smith preached to integrated audiences because white holiness believers felt Smith's power and flocked to gatherings to hear her preach.

Smith was also a singer and a missionary. She founded an orphanage. However, Smith's ministry faced two key obstacles. She was female and Black. She felt people would identify with the problems Blacks endured if they could be Black for 24 hours. Despite facing discrimination and sexism, Smith preached and taught the word of God to thousands.

Several women scholars penned influential Christian writings. Catherine Booth, the wife of William Booth, published a pamphlet *Female Ministry in 1859* which defended female ministers by arguing that women have been instrumental in leading souls to Christ for centuries. Mary Cagle was ordained by the Church of the Nazarene, where her husband became a district superintendent and she became a district evangelist.

During the 19th century, several women founded holiness organizations. Alma White and her husband established the Pillar of Fire which grew out of the Pentecostal Union. She was consecrated as a bishop in 1918, making her the first woman bishop of a Christian denomination. She became the lead preacher over her husband and they eventually divorced. She introduced vegetarianism to her congregation. In her mid-fifties, she learned how to drive and obtained a New Jersey driver's license. During that time, driving was considered unladylike.

Alma White (1862-1946) Bain News Service
1st woman bishop of a Christian denomination 1918

    A holiness evangelist, Susie Stanley wrote in her autobiography that many scriptures proved Jesus worked with and affirmed women. It was Mary Magdalene who first saw and testified to the resurrection. Phoebe was a deacon in an early Christian church. Paul listed women church leaders in Romans 16 and other letters. Finally, she noted that Paul said in Galatians 3:28 that there was "neither male nor female, for ye are all one in Christ Jesus."[xi]

According to Phyllis Zagano, a religious scholar, St. Paul called Phoebe a deacon and not a deaconess of the church of Cenechrae. From the onset of the Roman Empire until now, Catholics have consistently opposed female religious leaders. Augustus (345-430 AD) had a far reaching negative influence on the treatment of women. He embraced marriage, but not celibacy. He embraced the old Roman idea that the father's role in the house demanded he inflict physical pain on their wives and children. Neither Luther nor Calvin gave any thought to the equality of women as persons. In the fourth century women became converts. They exercised their gifts of learning, teaching, and ministering under women.

In 2002, the International Theological Commission approved a study which supported excluding women from the diaconate. The question about women deacons was on the table for decades, and in 1974, the commission determined that the ordination of women was sacramental. Some claimed women were never ordained and never will be ordained.

Even though women of the early church were called deacons, eventually, a consensus flourished describing deacons as male. Cardinal Jean Danielou, a French Jesuit described four ministerial duties of women deacons which are as follows:

1. Evangelization, catechesis, and spiritual direction
2. Liturgical roles equivalent to porter, acolyte, lector, and deacon
3. Care of the sick, including anointing, and
4. Liturgical prayer

Today, the deaconess is considered one of the two

branches of the diaconate. At some point women were ordained to the diaconate in rituals similar to those used to ordain men. The bishop laid hands on each woman in the presence of the presbytery. A mid-eighth century ritual required women to be ordained by the bishop in the sanctuary. The commission claimed women deacons were ordained to the ministry rather than the priesthood which was used to justify excluding women from the clergy.

In 1985, the late Basil Cardinal Hume, Archbishop of Westminster and President of the Episcopal conferences of Europe, told an Italian journalist he would be happy if the church ordained women deacons. The Greek Orthodox Church ordained monastic deacons through the 1950s. There is an international interest in ordaining female deacons. Even through opponents against women clergy would 'beg to differ;' the author of *Holy Saturday* argued that women and men are ontologically equal.

During biblical times women played key roles in their communities. However, there was no question that males were dominant in society, especially their role in religion, government, and in the social order. Throughout history, those in power have been prone to dominate and oppress a lower class of its citizens. During the Mosaic era, the Egyptians enslaved the Israelites.

After Europeans conquered the Americas, society changed. Indian societies were matriarchal. When the United States of America was formed in 1776, it became a patriotic society like the rest of Europe. For nearly 100 years after its formation, only white males could vote. In 1870, the 14th Amendment to the Constitution gave newly freedmen the right to vote. But, they and their community remained the subjects of widespread inequity. Blacks in general earned less, suffered with higher unemployment than their white neighbors, and were required to follow unjust Jim Crows rules.

Susan B. Anthony, 1820-1906, Preacher, Women's Advocate
Courtesy of the Library of Congress.

In 1848 women in the United States organized the Women's Rights and Suffrage Movement. The religious social order in the United States of America was layered too. Author William B. Booth reported that during the 19th century, blacks were required to worship in the balcony of the churches and were restricted to a special time to pray and kneel at the communion table. In some states, women could not own property by themselves, so their property was placed in their husband's names. In addition, even after women obtained voting rights in 1920, American society reserved submissive and subordinate occupational and social roles for them.

However, unlike modern male preachers, Jesus accepted women as his closest followers. In the Gospel of John, there were seven episodes recorded of Jesus' encounters with women which included the miracle of Cana, the apprehension of the adulterous woman, the death of Lazarus, the anointment of feet before the Passover, the crucifixion, and the resurrection in the garden.

Jesus was concerned about the welfare of all including children, women, the young, the old, the rich, the poor, the handicapped, the enslaved, and the disenfranchised. He was also in the business of releasing captives, and He nurtured great relationships with women. In the past two centuries, women preachers faced numerous social obstacles. However, modern women broke the veil and began to use their gifts to preach and teach the gospel increasingly after they obtained voting rights. By then, there were reportedly more than 3,000 women ministers and preachers in America.[xii]

Modern women preachers stand on the shoulders of activists who fought for women's rights. Many scholars attribute the social advancement of women with the Feminist Movements. A feminist is a person who respects the rights of every individual, whether male or female. Jesus has been dubbed a humanitarian as well as a feminist. Jesus tried to get the Jewish community to embrace change. He was constantly defying the old norms. By His example, He showed that society changes in time. History had shown us all - nothing remains the same.

Because of the rigid thinking of men, from the 1800s until WWII, very little progress was made in terms of women breaking the glass ceiling into obtaining preaching positions. However, by the late 20th century and the onset of the 21st century, women began to make progress toward obtaining key teaching and preaching positions when they completed their divinity studies at seminaries.

From 1800 -1970, women struggled to get from the church pews to the pulpit which is the highest role of authority in the church. There is no doubt about it, the women's liberation movement paved the way.

Women preachers of great status such as Lucretia Collins Mott, Elizabeth Cady Stanton, Lucy Stone Blackwell, and Susan B. Anthony, who were never ordained as ministers by their church, preached and paved the way for modern women preachers. They preached during an era when women were treated like children by their husbands in their homes.

Today, the winds of change have rendered women active teachers in seminaries. In fact, women teach eight out of 10 seminary classes. By the 1900s, women opened the cracked door to the ministry a litter wider.

TWO

Famous Female Preachers/Feminists: 1800 – 1970

If the man may preach, because the Savior died for him, why not the woman? seeing He died for her also. Is He not a whole Saviour, instead of a half one?

Jarena Lee, 1836

When Jarena Lee, a female evangelist, approached Rev. Richard Allen and asked his blessing to ordain her as a Baptist minister he refused, claiming the Baptist discipline did not call for women preachers. Allen was accustomed to giving a rallying cry to his congregation for the justice of Blacks, but he overlooked his own sexist views. Allen refused to ordain Lee even after witnessing she had been called by God.

Male clergy simply felt a woman's place was that of a wife, a mother, and a person secondary to men. Lee retorted, "And why should it be thought impossible, heterodox, or improper for a woman to preach, seeing the Savior died for woman as well as the man."[xiii]

African America pulpiteers are guilty of attempting to take the racist beam out of White America's eyes while ignoring the sexist beam in their eyes. Even though the scripture can be misinterpreted, passages in the bible confirm God gave His blessing for women to preach.

For example, Acts 2:17-18 states God intends to use all of his forces in the last days to put the kingdom's agenda before a dying world. Sons and daughters, young men and old men, both men and women, are candidates for the outpouring of the Holy Spirit and the preaching assignment. When Paul wrote the church in Rome, his letter addressed 29 of his co-workers in the ministry; ten of them were women.

However, in reference to Timothy, when he was in Corinth, he was dealing with a troubled congregation. It is worth noting, Timothy engaged with women in ministries in other areas. Timothy's strongest support was from the church at Philippi which was organized by Lydia and had been founded by women and led by businesswomen. Priscilla was mentioned in Romans 16:3; she is the same co-worker who worked with Paul as a tentmaker along with her husband.

Advocates for Women's Rights

Women refused to remain silent and lifted their voices to advocate for social and economic equality. Rev. Michelle Cobb was barred from the pulpit by the Baptist Church. However, she became the pastor of a United Methodist Church and an outstanding advocate for women's rights. She made the following statement about her experience:

> O Children of God and joint heirs of Christ, remember that Christ is too big to be bound by our biases; that Christ is too powerful to be imprisoned by our prejudices; that Christ is too great to be garrisoned by our little

games; that Christ is too wonderful to be walled in our small worlds; and that Christ is too splendid to be saddled with our sexist baggage.

Let's lift the Savior up for women and men to see, and He's promised, if I, if I be lifted up from the earth, I'll draw all men, all women, all ages, all classes, all regions, and all nations unto me. Our Lord woos and calls whomever he wills, and he does not need us to make the motion or to offer the second or to cast a vote on whom He calls. Let's leave the calling to Him; and the door to ministry will swing wide for women; and what is more, His will shall be done on earth as it is in heaven."[xiv]

A Massachusetts Quaker woman, Abby Kelley Foster, participated in the first women's rights convention in Seneca Falls, New York in 1848. While in Cleveland, she discussed her disappointment with the outcomes of America's Declaration of Independence which had overlooked and excluded women. She also addressed the Fourth National Woman's Rights Convention in Cleveland, Ohio in 1853. She lifted her voice over public sentiment against American women by pointing her finger to the male clergy. She reasoned that the clergy was responsible for the ultimate legal and public opinion against women because they were charged with the task of educating the common mind.

Foster retorted that anointed men speak of the moral duty of God and man. Nineteenth century clergymen influenced the manners and morals of citizens residing in urban and rural communities. Preachers molded the beliefs and behaviors of the nation. Even though the press became popular during this time, it was secondary to the power of men in the pulpit.

As it is a well-known, persuasion requires having

something to say and a place to say it. Early female activists had problems finding a platform to use their voice. Women had to create a platform before they could argue for social, political, and religious status. The Declaration of Sentiment and Resolutions of the 1848 conference urged women to "overthrow the monopoly of the pulpit."

Abby Kelley Foster 1811-1887
Photo Courtesy of the Library of Congress
Quaker, Abolitionist, Women's Rights Advocate

Men forbid the public speaking of women in this era. In 1838, a public address by a woman in Philadelphia sparked a riot. When the rioters calmed down the meeting hall had been destroyed. Hence, social change for women was hindered because they were silenced and had no platform to persuade males to give them equal rights.

Phoebe Palmer (1807-1874) was a popular evangelist, a writer, and one of the most profound voices seeking to overthrow the church monopoly. She was not an ordained minister, but she was one of the most popular and widely read evangelists of her time. In 1859, she published *The Promise of the Father* in hopes of influencing church leaders to support women's right to speak in public and to witness their faithfulness to God. Her premise was based on the spiritual equality of men and women.

A quote from *The Promise of the Father* detailed her views on the rights of women to be included in the clergy:

> Women are often led to proclaim the word of the Lord among us…Nor is there anything astonishing or novel in this particular direction of the Holy Spirit. Nothing astonishing, because there is no respect of persons with God. The soul of the woman, in his sight, is as the soul of man; and both are alike susceptible of the extraordinary as well as the general influences of the Spirit.
>
> Phoebe Palmer
The Promise of the Father (66-67)

Scholars claimed early feminists identified personhood and womanhood upon which to base their appeal for women's rights. Personhood was based on natural law which proposed men and women were ultimately the same and shared a common humanity. Based on this premise, women argued they should be given the same rights as men.

The appeal to womanhood was rooted on the difference between nature, and the role of men and women, and the superiority of women. Because women are superior to men, women should be granted an increased public role and rights for the betterment of society.

William Lloyd Garrison, 1805-1879, May 20. 1854
Garrison published the anti-slavery newspaper, *The Liberator*

While women writers uplifted the strengths of woman, many books authored by males demeaned women. The book, *Cult of True Womanhood*, described women as weak, gentle, and passive while men were characterized as strong, competitive, and ruthless. Women were considered quiet and demure. They were presumed too passive and too timid for the public arena and the cut-throat marketplace, both of which were reserved for men. Women were perceived as nurturing and loving; their qualities were best suited for the private domestic sphere of their home and family.

According to societal stereotypes, authentic women were timid and fragile, and were required to remain quiet in church leaving the preaching to the men. The cultural descriptions of women were designed to exclude them from all public activities including the platform, pulpit, and the polling place. The theological argument proposed God was the head of the universe. He assigned separate spheres for men and women. Men were the earthly heads of families and nations, and women were obedient and silent keepers of the earth.

Based on Genesis, men argued women were created after and out of man which deemed them inferior to man. Biologically, men reasoned that women were emotional, illogical, and prone to hysteria. Their constitution of nervousness left them vulnerable to fainting, a claim Sojourner Truth refuted at the 1848 Women's Conference.

Some also inferred that women had small brains and lacked intelligence. One Harvard professor concluded that women were not suitable for higher education. He said,

> ...their brains presumably were too small to sustain the

rational deliberation required in politics and business... Harvard medical professor Dr. Edward Clarke (1873) argued against higher education for women on the grounds that the blood needed to sustain development or the ovaries and womb would be diverted to the brain which he believed was a major cause of serious illness.[xv]

The women's rights movement was modeled after the anti-slavery movement which was rooted in the religious doctrine claiming the belief of equality for all human beings in the sight of God. A group of churches organized the movement, notably the Quakers, who supported human freedom. Historian William L. O'Neil claimed religion formed the cornerstone of the case against women's rights.

Nationally, ministers supported the notion that women should play a role in forming religious character for their family; but, their leadership could not go outside of the threshold of their homes. Samuel J. May and William H. Channing were Unitarian clergymen who supported women's suffrage. Channing was a great advocate for human rights and he circulated a petition calling for women's right to freedom, representation, and suffrage.

Theodore Parker declared, "A woman has the same human nature that a man has... The same human rights, to life, liberty, and the pursuit of happiness; the same human duties; and they are as inalienable in a woman as in a man." Rev. James Freeman Clarke expressed that women should be given the opportunity to explore new spheres of duty. "If a woman wants to study medicine, let her study it; if she wants to study divinity, let her study it; if she finds faculties within her, let them have a chance to expand"[xvi]

Author Ella P. Mitchell pointed out that in Luke 12:54-

56, Jesus said to the multitude, "When you see a cloud rising in the west, you say at once, 'A shower is coming' and so it happens. And when you see the south wind blowing, you say, 'There will be scorching heat,' and it happens. You hypocrites! You know how to interpret the appearance of earth and sky; but why do you not know to interpret the present?" With women in ministry in mind, why do some know how to interpret the present time?[xvii]

Mitchell proclaimed that God is calling women and filling them with the living Word and trying to get men to see them as God sees them. When Jeremiah was called to the ministry, he told God he was too young for the job. God told Jeremiah that He knew him before he formed him in his mother's wound. God told Jeremiah He had known him longer than he knew himself and God was trying to get Jeremiah to see himself as God saw him. As Jesus called us to watch the signs of the times centuries ago, today Mitchell announced that "women are on fire, under fire."[xviii]

In the words of Miriam Winter, an advocate for women preachers, she wrote:

> Two women care,/ four women dare, and ten will follow after. /Two are few, but four are more,/ and ten times worth waiting for./ A million strong on a single song,/ and the whole world sings along,/ and a new day dawns./ Out there on your own,/ know that you are not alone./ Look around and see / signs of solidarity./ When you feel harassed, / first in line, yet always last, / don't withdraw and hide./ Find a friend to stand after. / Two are few, but four are more, / and ten times ten worth waiting for./ A million strong on a single song, / soon the whole world sings along, / a new day dawns."[xix]

A former slave who played a pivotal role in the abolition of slavery and woman's rights was Sojourner Truth. Truth became a spiritual orator, and a travelling preacher. Truth and Harriet Tubman were the most famous black women in the 19th century.

Truth was born in 1797 in rural New York. In her adult life, Truth went from camp meetings to lecture hall preaching, teaching, lecturing, and singing Methodist hymns and songs which she created. Sojourner Truth was a six-foot-tall dark-skinned woman, who dressed like a Quaker. She always wore a turban. She often stabbed the air with her fingers as she expressed her disapproval of causes she opposed. Truth's power over audiences was compared to French classical tragedienne Mademoiselle Rachel who was one of the most popular actresses of the time.

Sojourner Truth, the second of 12 or 13 children to James and Elizabeth in Ulster County, New York, was born Isabella. In the fall of 1826, Isabella took her infant daughter, Sophia, with her, leaving her other children behind, and walked to freedom. New York had established an emancipation law which excluded her children because they had been born after 1799. Walking away from slavery was her first act of liberation. Then, she had a revelation from God that He was omnificent. She became empowered by her religious faith even though she was a poor, black, woman.

From 1828 to 1843, Sojourner Truth was a passionate member of the Methodist Church. She performed mission work and attended camp meetings. On June 1, 1843, Isabella left New York to go east to lecture. It was at this point that she changed her name to Sojourner Truth. She was illiterate, but learned the bible by having people read to her; she was wise and had a strong will to learn God's words. She preferred for children to read to her because they didn't mind reading pages repeatedly; the repetition helped her learn better. Plus, she possessed a great memory.

Sojourner Truth, 1826 to 1883
© 1864 by Sojourner Truth. LC-USZC4-6165

While a resident of Northampton Association of Education and Industry, a Utopian cooperative community, she met William Lloyd Garrison, Frederick Douglass, George Thompson, Wendell Phillips, and David Ruggles, a Negro editor of an antislavery newspaper. From her association with these great orators and activists, Truth became familiar with the anti-slavery and the woman's rights movement.

Frederick Douglass, 1818–1895, age 62
Social reformer, abolitionist, *The North Star*, Publisher
by George Francis Schreiber, April 26, 1870, LC-USZ62-15887

Eliza Leggett, who advocated for women's suffrage, described Truth as a woman with a potent public persona. "Those who have heard Sojourner will never forget her power, never forget how they sway'd wit her will – she caught on her Staff, her tall figure bent a little with ever looking keen and tender yet pitiful – a far off look as tho' she caught the future, then rising she would … speak in words so searching, so true, that pale faces would brighten and flush in response.[xx] Truth was remembered for saying, "And aint' I a woman." She spoke in broken slave dialect. A portion of one of her speech follows:

> Dat man over dar say dat woman need to be helped into carriages, and lifted over ditches, and to have de best eberwhar. Nobody eber helps me into carriages, or ober mud-puddles, or gives me any best place, [and, raising herself to her full height, and her voice to a pitch like rolling thunder, she asked], "And aint' I am women? Look at me! Look at my arm! "I have plowed and planted and gathered into barns, and no man could head me – and aint' I a woman? I could work as much and eat as much as a man when I could get it and bear de lash as well – aint' I a woman? I have borne thirteen children and seen em' mos all sold off into slavery, and when I cried out with a mother's grief, none by Jesus heard – and aint' I a woman? Den day talks bout dis ting in de head—what dis day call it? ["Intellect," whispered some one near.] "Dat's it, honey. What's dat got to do with women's rights? If my cup won't hold but a pint and yourn holds a quart, wouldn't ye be mean not to let me have my little half-measure full?[xxi]

Sojourner Truth placed her faith in God, and used her

voice to advance women's liberation and the right for all humans to freedom. Her powerful oratory rendered her a Champion for her race and the rights of women.

President Lincoln showing Sojourner Truth the Bible presented by colored people of Baltimore, Executive Mansion, Washington, D.C., Oct. 29, 1864 – Presidential file LC-USZ62-16225
Photograph of painting R.D. Bayley 1893

Despite her age, Truth worked tirelessly to take supplies to Negro volunteer regiments during the Civil War. In 1864, she went to Washington D.C. and protested until they integrated street cars. She talked to President Abraham Lincoln while there. She accepted an appointment with the National Freedman's Relief Association where she counseled ex-slaves about resettling.

Truth moved to Washington in 1854 and worked in the Freedman's hospital. In the spirit of our Lord and Savior, Truth and others dedicated their lives to helping the least of God's children. They allowed God's light to shine here on earth through their deeds. Isn't that worth a lot? Truth and other women dedicated their lives preaching and speaking to small gatherings, to small groups, and at public forums.

Truth and others led women's liberation advancements many years ago. By the 21st century, woman had broken the glass ceiling in sports, education, politics, and religion. Their gains were prompted by voices that walked miles to speak to anyone willing to listen and whose voices, writings, speeches, songs, and prayers reached the clergy, the politicians, and men who kept closing the door while women stood on the other side.

THREE

Modern Women Stand in the Pulpit

At the onset of the 21st century, church doors opened wider to women clergy. After the 1970s women become ordained ministers in greater numbers. After a decade of struggle, the Protestant mainline churches began ordaining women in the mid-1970s. Today, women comprise around 11 percent of the nation's clergy.[xxii] The longstanding stained-glass ceiling against allowing women to enter the pulpit was based on prejudices that kept women from leading and being given the opportunity to shape the faith of others.

According to the Association of Theological Schools in Pittsburg, Pennsylvania, the percentage of women studying in seminaries in 1972 was 10.2, in 1982 it was 23.7, and in 1995 it had reached 32.8.[xxiii] The number of African American women studying theology had increased as well, but they only comprised fewer than five percent of pastors in U.S. churches. Regardless of the rigid force to keep women out of the pulpit, the glass ceiling is slowly closing.

Only a few churches including the Quakers; the Christian Connection Church, now known as the United Church of Christ; and the Wesleyan Holiness ordained women in the 19th century. The Presbyterian Church USA and the United Methodist Church first ordained women in 1956.

From 1971 to 1980, women entered seminaries in unprecedented numbers. The Evangelist Lutheran Church granted full clergy rights to women in 1970, and the Episcopal Church ordained them in 1976. The unprecedented ordainment of women during the 1970s produced substantial gains in the following years.

Ordaining women into the priesthood is permitted under church law, but research revealed there is a large disparity between formal acceptance of women and actual women priests. Overall, there remains a long way to go in terms of women achieving full equality to men. A 1996 study showed that more responsible and prestigious church positions are given disproportionately to men. As one woman said, "Ordination is one thing; deployment is another."[xxiv]

Many newly elected Episcopalian bishops are fully supportive of women in the clergy; the number opposing women in the clergy are declining as those holding biases against women retire. The first woman was elected bishop in 1989. She said, "Now I am no longer an oddity as a woman rector… There is a movement forward… It's not as quick as I'd like. I suppose it never is, but there is a major change. Societal pressure for women to obtain equality has reached universal cultural hegemony."[xxv]

The Episcopal Clerical Directory of 1999 reported that of a total of 17,117 ordained clergy, 14,077 were men, and 3,040 were women. Those ordained included priests and deacons. Prior to 1977, the Episcopal Church virtually had not ordained any women. In 1976, men held 100 percent and women held 0 percent of the positions in the churches. By

1978, only 15 percent were women; by 1984 that number had doubled to 30 percent. By the mid-1980s, women tenures had declined, and by the 1990s, they had stabilized.

1Timothy 3:2 states, "A bishop must have one wife." The rest of the scripture says a bishop, "must be blameless, vigilant, sober, of good behavior, given to hospitality, apt to teach." Many argue a woman can possess these qualifications. Of course, there are those who still do not get it.

In the scripture, God allowed women to prophesy, which is an indication that He intended to use women to spread His word; one of God's messengers proclaimed that women were to remain silent. However, this interpretation of the scripture was inaccurate for the bible says man in the general sense of humanity which does not stipulate that it can't be a woman and it further says in 1 Corinthians 14: 27, 28 "If any man speak in an unknown tongue, let one interpret. But if there be no interpreter, let him keep silence in the church."

Therefore, the use the term man doesn't eliminate the possibility of it referring to a woman. The scripture indicated that on certain issues even men were asked to 'keep silent.'

Preaching is defined: "To bring or declare, good, or glad, tidings, to proclaim, to be a herald." These terms don't seem specific or mandatory only for a man to follow. Paul commanded women not to have authority over men, and the question for us today is whether it is culturally applicable to us now.

1 Timothy stated that a woman remain silent not to have reign over a man. Well, there are plenty of women, men, and children who need to be uplifted, taught, and edified.

Obstacles that Women Clergy Face

To discuss women preachers, we must explore pre-qualifications in the bible and in society. Again, there are the prejudices of men who view women as incapable of preaching and having authority to oversee men. There are prolific roles in rearing male children, students and community rehabilitation and restructuring.

Unity is a source of powerful production to transform a flawed society. Both parents are a teaching unit for their offspring. Women are the spiritual powerhouse that carry the woes of the world so who better to uplift the spirit through God's Word than women. Progress was being made in 1979 to accept the diversity of our American culture.

How women redefined traditional roles is a challenge worth pursuing. In 1956, when full clergy rights were granted to women their own path had been blocked despite their accomplishment of graduating from seminary school. Later, she gained access to the membership she so longed to be granted.

The Methodist approved ordination of women in 1956, and the Presbyterian followed suit in 1964. The American Lutheran Church and the Southern Baptist Church awarded rights in 1970 to women ministries. The Protestant followed suit in 1976, but the Episcopal denomination fought with aggressive resistance. There are always exceptions to the rule.

In 1853, there were only 380 fully ordained women preachers in America through the United Methodist. In the 1980's, the Protestant's record revealed there were 3,200 ordained women clergy. People of religious merit and strength stand up for the flaws in society purging forward to take the winding road; the higher road moving on up a steep climb is just what Judith Weidman, a religious scholar, tackled.

Though early indications seem to suggest that the influence of the women's movement has been felt largely through changes in the general environment Weidman suggested that women's ordination was possibly an offset of the feminist movement.[xxvi]

Weidman's research mentioned how different denominations faced various issues; for example, the Episcopal persuasion denoted that the Priest was viewed as a representative of Christ, and a strong male image has been a central image to them. Therefore, it was difficult for them to accept women's ordination in the ministry.

In 1977, a program called the Women in Ministry under the United Presbyterian Church was created with a budget of $500,000 to open general acceptance to women in the pulpit. Chapter 10 focused on Lora Gross who spoke of the embodied church and devised a model to propose her vision of women in the church. The General Convention of the Episcopal Church approved the ordination of women at its 1976 meeting.

Scholar James Nelson's thesis was based on whether there is an interconnection between human sexuality and the broken relationship among human beings that is at the very root of social injustice. He described the "higher self and fleshy life," wherein our conceptual world becomes populated with dichotomies: for example, good/bad, heterosexual/homosexual, and male/female.

A 1980 study suggested that it takes women clergy longer to find jobs because congregations are more unwilling to hire women. Also, women clergy are less likely referred through placement agencies. As a result, women tended to seek or settle for secular work. In addition, the first job became a relevant factor on future career options. A study conducted by U.S. Catholic noted, "It thus seems more likely that characteristics such as sex, age, or race will act as a sorting mechanism in this search process than in later searches."

Researchers mailed 7,000 questionnaires; half of the responses desired the research to focus on parishes and 2,183 responses determined it focus on ministry. The study researched 15 denominations; three hundred interview follow ups showed that 55 percent of those who become employed were men compared to 42 percent of women. Within 24 months, 81 percent of men as opposed to 67 percent of women became gainfully employed. Whereas in the first 104 days, 50 percent of men were employed; in comparison, it took women 225 days to achieve the same level of employment.[xxvii]

United Methodist exhibited the smallest sex difference; their policy mandated full employment for all ordained clergy regardless of gender. During the 1970's, men gained positions and appointments very rapidly versus women in their first 90 days at a ratio of 50 percent compared to 20 percent for women. Yet, after five months it was 62 percent to 30 percent men to women. The hazard rates increased; still women have much lower career placement rates which was 21 percent less.

Mississippi's plight of tackling the racial and gender placement of women in the ministry is very interesting. Rev. Amzie Cotton, a preacher of Greater True Vine Holmes Church, supported the ordination of women in 1984 at the Mississippi Baptist Convention. Upon his advancement to bishop, his wife, Mary, became his predecessor. "Women have been laboring in the gospel for a long time. It is hypocritical to say God did not call women to the ministry," he reasoned. Therefore, Cotton established the Amzie Cotton School of Ministry so it could train and license women ministers.

In 1975, after his work in civil rights in 1960's, Bishop Gray indoctrinated women into the priesthood. The prolific words of Rev. Colton Smith represented the ordination of women; he declared that "[a] priest at the altar represents all humanity not just the male half."

The churchmen for Apostle Faith and Order spoke daringly strong against female preachers reasoning that preaching requires total devotion, not women out of their minds talking erratically. He called the pastors' ordination of woman insane and eccentric.

The ordination of women will prevail with perseverance, and eventually the gap will close. In the book *Religion in Mississippi*, Mississippi Baptists denied women's ordination at the State convention leaving the option open for each individual church. During the convention, traditional family, societal issues, community perspectives, and biblical laws and scripture were discussed. Clergy debated whether the parish should allow women preachers. Society always promotes change; but, some resist it with full force.

John Thomason argued that the Bible was written in a patriarchal culture but that Jesus accepted the ministry of women. In 1991, Marian Young Talley and Ida Allen were the first two women ordained in an integrated Baptist congregation under the appointment of Reverend Bill Patrick who stated, "How can I question what God calls [them] to do?"[xxviii]

The Catholic Church agreed with the views of Fundamentalists on issues such as antiabortion. However, Rev. Cullen of St. Richard Catholic Church expressed, "It's dangerous to mix dogmatic religious approach to something that's a cultural or social problem."

He also spoke on antifeminism, but it was hypocritical for 100 women to meet upon their very own doorstep shortly before he proposed this claim. Rosner Barwick chaired the gathering at St. Richards and delivered the women's request to be part of the decision-making process. She stated, "Women wanted to be considered as thinking entities."[xxix]

Richard Brogan outlined a theological basis that echoed the Egalitarian spirit of the early evangelicals based on theology that emphasized the unity of the human family, the universality of God's love, and the redemptive power of faith.

The theory of power and gender is drawn up as such: powerless women identify through powerless men, but powerless men and women both identify with empowered women. We have so many social and spiritual issues, but they all require our full combined attention and devotion to all human beings, each serving their individual purpose whether they are male or female.

FOUR

Popular Women Preachers

In April of 2000, Anne Graham Lotz, the daughter of a world renown preacher, Rev. Billy Graham, addressed a crowd of 12,500 at the University of Tennessee's Thompson-Boling Arena in Knoxville. In June of 2000, while Lotz represented a new era of evangelists, the Southern Baptist Convention was planning to bar women from the pulpit at its annual meeting. No one could dispute that she was reaching lost souls. Her world revival tour was filling 25,000 seat arenas.

Her popularity was becoming a big challenge to those who refused to ordain women preachers. She had become the best-known female evangelist in the U.S. *The New York Times* named Lotz one of the five possible candidates to take over her father's place when he retired.

When the Southern Baptist Convention met in Orlando, Florida, it was expected to add a clause to the Baptist Faith and Message stating: "While both men and women are gifted for service in the church, the office of pastor is limited to men as qualified by Scripture." At that time, there were roughly 100 women leading Baptist congregations; however, the clause would prevent women from being ordained in the future. At the convention, Lotz referred to herself as a 'bible expositor' instead of a preacher.

The Baptist Church is the largest U.S. Protestant denomination. Its rejection of women preachers clashes with existing trends toward women breaking the glass ceiling

Billy Graham, 1918- April 11, 1966
Courtesy of the Library of Congress

into the pulpit. The Lutherans, Episcopalians, and Methodists allow women to preach from the pulpit, even though few women have obtained leadership roles over large congregations.

Lotz did not complete seminary, and does not have a college education, and she chose not to be ordained; but, she believes women have the right to be ordained. Lotz considers herself a teacher, but she does not identify as a feminist. She has written award winning books and preached to tens of thousands of people. When Lotz first launched her ministry, her famous parents were not enthusiastic about it. After hearing her preach in 1983, Rev. Billy Graham described it as a stunning display which captured the attention of the gathered assembly.

Some men publicly complained about Lotz preaching after her revivals. She replied to their complaints, "I went to the Scripture, and I had to really pray that through, and God was very clear. Men could come and be on the periphery and be blessed. God would be there for them, but they were not to be the target. I read John 4, where Jesus reaches Samaria through one woman at the well."[xxx]

Lotz said she doesn't want to be a preacher or a senior pastor. She explained, "I just want to present the gospel, and I do it in an arena, not in a church building." Lotz was once told by an African pastor who heard her preach that God spoke to him while she was preaching. He was stunned because he received a revelation through a woman. He decided to go back home and tell his church in Africa that God speaks through sisters.

Barbara Brown Taylor, an Episcopalian priest, is another popular preacher. She was named one of 12 most effective preachers in the English-speaking world. Taylor is a well-known dynamic preacher. Since she was ordained in 1984, she has inspired thousands of listeners. Taylor said, "There are geniuses, people with a real gift. But it would be a mistake to be discouraged by their example because it's also possible to learn to be a good preacher."[xxxi]

Taylor said when she was sitting in the pews she heard so many baseball and golf stories. Now diapering and cooking have made it into the pulpit, to the point you can see some guys rolling their eyes. But she feels feminine stories have really added more life in church. She believes narcissism should be excluded from sermons.

Taylor argued that sermons should connect to human experiences, and she condemned those pastors who make their sermons personal. "Have you ever wondered… or Once upon a time there was a man…,"[xxxii] are great opening line, but she argued starting with 'I' disconnects the pastor from the audience. Overall, Taylor believes sermons should try to feed the head, heart, and will. Eventually, she left the ministry to teach at Piedmont College in rural northeast Georgia, but she continues to move audiences with her powerful message.

Black women have been seeking equal opportunities for centuries; however, they have slowly gained equality in the church. Black woman, especially, have been limited to the church roles of missionaries, musicians, choir directors, church secretaries, etc. By the early 1980s, an estimated 1,000 black women were leading their own congregations.[xxxiii]

One Black preacher, Rev. Dorothy Love Pearson, was called to the ministry in 1957, but she had to change her denomination to become an ordained minister. She was the pastor of Mt. Olive Baptist Church. She passed at age 82 in

2015. Rev. Elizabeth Doles was appointed pastor of Martin Chapel A.M.E. Zion in 1969. At that time, the church had less than a dozen members. Since then the church has grown considerably.

Rev. Trudie Trimm she became the first black women to be ordained among the 27,000 pastors affiliated with the National Baptist Convention. She was the pastor of one of the largest churches in Chicago, Illinois. She was called into the minister in 1965 when her husband died. Rev. Carolyn Tyler was ordained the pastor of First A.M.E. Church in Indio, California in 1977.

The majority of Southern Baptists shunned women leadership for many years, and numerous African American males have been twice as closed minded. Rev. Mary Moore, the pastor of New Salem Missionary Baptist Church in south Memphis, Tennessee has met her share of male chauvinism and ridicule from inside and outside of the African American community.

According to Memphis Theological Seminary, only a few black women attended seminary in the 1960s and 1970s, but today the number has increased to 15 percent. When faced with opposition to preach, some black women simply have organized their own churches. Although African American women have made some strides, by far, they have a tougher road ahead.

A 1998 study showed that women were often confined to specialized ministries such as music, youth, and bible study. Many women pastors were serving as associate pastors. Carroll conducted a study which showed that 20 percent of women were the lead or solo pastors of congregations. However, only three percent of women are pastors at the top of the pay scale over mega churches. One percent of women lead conservative Protestant churches. Of African American churches, only three percent are women.[xxxiv]

Unfortunately, research has shown that the demographic image of a pastor has not changed much since the 1950s. Congregations want a young married man with children. Smaller, poorer congregations will hire female pastors, but when a senior pastor develops a list of eligible persons he recommends succeeding, there usually aren't any women on his list. Women in African American Protestant churches can serve as itinerant evangelists, but rarely as pastors.

Vashti McKenzie was elected the first female bishop in the history of the African Methodist Episcopal (A.M.E.) Church. She reigned over its 18th district which included the churches in Lesotho, Swaziland, Botswana, and Mozambique. A cloud of uncertainty hung over her head when she was assigned to a 300-member church in the state of Maryland in 1990, but McKenzie proved her value to the ministry.

Under her leadership, the membership increased from 300 to 1,700. She was a trailblazer; she worked with the state to get 600 people in her community off welfare, saved a public school, and renovated a local building. In 2000, she launched and won a campaign to become bishop. Eventually she became the president of the A.M.E.'s Council of Bishops, where she started a program to build group homes for orphaned children affected with AIDS.

In 2002, Sarah Jackson Shelton was appointed senior pastor of the Baptist Church of the Covenant in Birmingham, becoming one of a few female Southern Baptists preachers in Alabama. During her first week on the job, two of her member's application to do missionary work in Swaziland was denied because the International Mission's Board refused to sign a belief statement with Shelton's church on the grounds that women should not teach or have authority over men. A representative of the mission's board said, "We can't tell a church who to hire, but by the same token, that woman's church cannot tell the Mission Board who it can send on its mission."[xxxv]

By 1992, the Church of England approved women priests, breaking 19 centuries of tradition. From 1972 to 2007, the number of women studying in seminaries went from 4.7 percent to 31 percent. The Presbyterian Church (USA) as well as old mainline Protestant communions have ordained women for decades. Nevertheless, none of them have become senior pastors in 'tall-steeple' churches.

Many conservative denominations do not ordain women and they are exempt on First Amendment grounds from complying with federal equal-opportunity laws. Women have struggled to get from the pew to the pulpit, in part, because male clergy fear that feminization of the clergy will make men leave the pews.

According to Jackson W. Carroll, Professor Emeritus of Religion and Society, Duke University Divinity School, and author of *God's Potters: Pastoral leadership and the shaping of congregations*, 70 percent of men become pastors of medium or large congregations in their second decade of ministry. However, only 37 percent of women become leaders of medium and large congregation.

Do you agree? Popular women preachers like McKenzie, Lotz, and Taylor have proved with the mere size of their audiences that God calls women to preach to lost souls.

FIVE

The Future of Women in Ministry

Let Charlie Lee-Potter, a researcher, tell it, the opponents of the ordination of women have lost the war. Research on the Church of England confirmed that 50 percent of those entering training to become priest are women. The Church of England started ordaining women in 1992. Since the turn of the 21st century, women make up 20 percent of the clergy. The Oxford diocese supplies more priests to the Church of England than any other area of the country. In England today, over 80 percent of the students are female. Research predicts women will become a majority of the church's clergy.

There has definitely been a shift in power toward empowering women clergy. The Northamptonshire village will be hiring a new vicar and all six of the applicants are women. Father Geoffrey Kirk, a proponent of the anti-female-priest association put it this way, "Very soon the priesthood will be seen as a hobby for grannies."[xxxvi]

Despite opposition, women are breaking the glass ceiling and gradually entering the highest job posts for clergy. Rev. Katherine Jefferts Schori, a 52-year-old Bishop in Nevada, made history by becoming the first woman to achieve the status of archbishop. According to the Episcopal Church, The Most Rev. Katherine Jefferts Schori became the 26th Presiding Bishop of the Episcopal Church in 2006. As such, she is over 2.1 million members in 17 countries, 108 dioceses... 38 Anglican Provinces. The American Episcopal Church began ordaining women in 1989.

Women are obtaining a little more parity with males each year, but there are still hurdles for them to climb in other professions. There are far more female clergy than surgeons, lawyers, and architects. In medicine, 70 percent of those graduating from medical school are women, but they only comprise seven percent of consultant surgeons. Forty-five percent of secondary school teachers are male, and they make up 65 percent of head teachers' posts.

Alysa Stanton is a clergy newsmaker. She became the first African American Rabbi in recorded history on June 6, 2009. Stanton completed seven years of training at Hebrew Union College, a Jewish Institute of Religion in Cincinnati. She was ordained by Rabbi David Ellenson. He said, "[Her] history-making journey reflects her profound commitment to Jewish learning and leadership. She brings to her rabbinate an infinite capacity for human understanding..."[xxxvii]

Hoffman's belief in Judaism was unusual. She was raised by Christians in Cleveland, Ohio; the family later moved to Colorado. After completing high school, Stanton engaged in a self-study program and explored different religions. Then, she met Messianic Christians who practiced Judaism. She studied Judaism for two years and then completed the conversion process.

After her conversion, Stanton felt trapped between two

worlds. Her African American friends called her a traitor and she was not accepted by the Jewish community. The criticism and rejection prompted her to shut down, and she disassociated herself from the synagogue for a year. But Stanton admitted, "I realized for better or worse, I am a Jew and I will live and die a Jew. According to official records, Stanton is the first African American female rabbi to lead a majority white congregation.

Women are reaching for higher ground in religion, sports, and other occupations. They have made a lot of progress and have begun to break the glass ceiling in diverse career fields. The future of female clergy looks brighter with each passing year. They are preaching and teaching to small congregations and to large gathering. They are delivering the 'good news' to millions. They have been ordained as pastors, priests, and other forms of the clergy. On the other hand, whether they are ordained or not, women are reaching lost souls and spreading the love of God without fear. As Mahatma Gandhi said, "You cannot be crushed by something you do not fear."

CONCLUSION

Women have been struggling to get from the church pews and into the pulpit for centuries. Since the ancient world, women have played key roles as heads of their family, community, and in the church. Many of the women around Moses including his mother, his sister, and Pharaoh's daughter were leaders who helped carry out God's plan.

Miriam helped Moses and Aaron provide spiritual leadership to the children of Israel after their departure from Egypt. Miriam was a prophet who led the women in song and dance after the miracle of the Sea of Reeds. She also saved Moses and went to pharaoh's daughter and persuaded her to nurse Moses. Moses was the official leader of the people, but Miriam was loved by her people.

During the exodus, Aaron and Miriam criticized Moses and she was stricken with a leprous condition. She was stuck outside the camp for seven days. The people rebelled and refused to move forward until she was brought back to the camp. When she died, the people complained until she was properly buried. Miriam was a powerful leader who was loved and adored by her people. The people's love for Miriam was a testament to her leadership capacity.

Moses's mother was a leader. She rebelled against the Egyptian law which ordered all Hebrews to throw all male babies in the Nile. She defied the law and hid Moses for three months. Then, she built an ark-like cradle for him to float among the reeds on the edge of the river. When the pharaoh's daughter and her maid found the basket, they hid his identity and took care of him.

McGrath credited women with engineering the Exodus

which saved Israel. His statement is as follows:

> Hence, Israel's central tradition, the Exodus, does not begin with the great liberator Moses. Instead, a diverse group of women – Hebrew and Egyptian, slave and royal, young and old – act together as instruments of God's saving power. They cross lines of ethnicity, social standing, and age in the interest of Moses' life. It is the saving activity of women that heralds the beginning of Israel's freedom from bondage.[xxxviii]

Like the women in the book of Moses, Judith was another brave, woman, who helped liberate Israel. The book which described Judith was written around 100 years before the birth of Christ, but the story happened four hundred years before His birth. The town of Bethulia had been besieged by Assyrian forces, who were calling for the citizens to surrender. Judith, a devout widow, acts in the face of inescapable danger.

She disguised herself and dressed like a Grego-Roman; she walked through enemy lines and presented herself to Holofernes, the Assyrian commander. He found Judith very attractive, so he invited her to dine with him. After he became drunk, Judith decapitated him with his own sword and placed his head in a bag. A woman's bravery saved the Israelites from destruction by Assyrian force; so, they retreated.

Jael, a maiden, wooed Sisera, the Canaanite commander into her tent. While Sisera was asleep, Jael seized a weapon nearby and nailed Sisera's head to the ground and brought an end to Israel's oppression by the Canaanites. According to the code of ancient warfare, the death of a feared warrior by the hands of a woman was a humiliating blow to the Assyrians, which earned greater safety for Israel. Jael was praised in Judges 5:24, "Blessed be Jael by women."

The spirit of God is poured out on women as well as it is on men. God's messengers are here to change the world. The kingdom has already come, and the preachers and messengers are children of the ruler. God calls messengers, God moves them, and empowers them. God uses witnesses and goes with them. Those called by God are obligated to preach the Word to everyone in the world. Their strength comes from the One who calls them by name. He calls the people of God to be the people of God. Women, men, the young, and the old are witnesses for God.

For thousands of years, women have been instrumental in carrying out God's plan for salvation. Women were created to serve as well as be helpmates for men. Scripture denotes that in the order of things, God is first, then a man, and then his wife. Yet, man rendered women inferior to him.

Women were often silenced and diminished by a patriarchal system that placed men at the top of society and women at the bottom. Despite man's resistance to women as authority figures, women have always played central roles in religion.

Regardless of all the naysayers, today, there is a massive, global, and inclusive agenda to restore the status of women. The tide is shifting, and women are taking their rightful places in God's plan to restore salvation to lost souls.

BIBLIOGRAPHY

Banerjee, Neela. Clergywomen find hard path to pulpit. *N York Times,* (26 August 2006), 1A.

Biema, Van, Kauffman David et al. Rising above the stained-glass ceiling. *Time,* June 2004, 163 (*26*), 1-5.

Booth, William D. (2001). The open door for women preachers: Acts 2:17, 18; 21:9; Romans 10:15; Ephesians 4:11. *The Journal of Religious Thought, Pastor's Corner,* 108-115.

Bunce, Alan. (1996). Diversity makes its way to the pulpit. *Christian Science Monitor, 88 (219),* 1-4.

Hens-Piazza. (January, 2006). A women's place is in the bible. *U.S. Catholic,* 30-33.

Hoffman, Melody K. (July, 2009). 1st Black woman Rabbi's Journey to history, *Jet,* 16-18.

Hogan, Lucy Lind, (2000). Negotiating personhood, womanhood, and spiritual equality: Phoebe Palmer's defense of the preaching women, *ATQ,* 211-226.

The Holy Bible: King James Version. (1988). Iowa Falls, Iowa: World Bible Publishers.

Kent, Keri Wyatt. (2008). A Reverent Maverick. *Christianity Today,* 46-50.

Lee-Potter, Charlie. (June, 2006). It's a woman's job now. *New Statesman,* 30-32.

McGrath, Mark J. (June, 1993). Buried treasures: Rediscovering women's roles in the bible. *U.S. Catholic,* 58 (6), 6-13.

Mitchell, E.P. (1993). *Women: To preach or not to preach.* Valley, PA: Judson Press.

Ruether, Rosemary, R. (2005, September). Women ascend the pulpit. *USA Today,* 66-67.

Neela, Banerjee. (August, 2006). Clergywomen find hard path to bigger pulpit. *The New York Times,* 1-5.

Nelson, Thomas. (1983). Precious Bible Promises. Nashville, TN: Thomas Nelson Publishers.

Norment, Lynn. (June, 2004). In the male domain of pasturing: Women find success in the pulpit. *Ebony,* November 1981, 99-104.

Parker, Suzi. (February, 1999). For women, a steep climb to the pulpit. *Christian Science Monitor, 91* (48), 1-3.

Patrik, Jonsson. (2000). Baptist women, denied pulpit, fill stadiums. *Christian Science Monitor,* 92 *(137).*

Lee-Potter, Charlie. (2006). It's a women's job now. *New Statesman,* 30-32.

Sparks, Randy J. (2001). Religion in Mississippi. *United States of America: Mississippi Historical Society.*

Sullins, Paul. (2000). The Stained Glass Ceiling: Career Attainment for Women Clergy. 61 *(3),* 243-266.

Tait, Jennifer W. (April, 2004). "I Received my Commission from Him, Brother." *Christian History & Biography,* 82, 35-38.

Time Magazine. (1992). The pulpit barrier, 140 (*21*), 11.

Zagano, Phyllis. (February, 2003). Catholic women deacons. *America Magazine*, 9-11.

Zink-Sawyer, Beverly A. (2000). From preachers to suffragists: Enlisting the pulpit in the early Movement for Woman's Rights. *Union Theological Seminary and the Presbyterian School of Christian Education,* 193-209.

Weidman, Judith L. (1981). Women Ministers: How women are redefining traditional roles. New York, NY: Harper & Row.

Wortham, Anne. (2000). Sojourner Truth. *World & I,* 15 (*3*), 1-17.

U.S. Catholic. *Preacher Women.* May 23, 2007, 72 (*7*), 30-35.

INDEX

Adams, Abigail Smith 16-17, 21

Banerjee, Neela 20
Beecher, Catherine 16
Blackwell, Lucy Stone 31
Blannbekin, Agnes 18
Booth, William D. 19
Bosanquet, Mary 20

Carroll, Jackson W. 61
Crosby, Sarah 20

Doles, Rev. Elizabeth 61

Ellenson, Rabbi David 65

Gandhi, Mahatma 66
Graham, Billy 57-59

Hildegard of Bingen 17, 19
Huldah, 9

Julian of Norwich 15, 16

King Josiah, 9
Kirk, Father Geoffrey 64

Lee-Potter, Charlie 64
Lincoln, President Abraham 3, 44-45
Lotz, Anne Graham 14
Lyon, Mary 16

Mademoiselle Rachel 41

Magdalene, Mary 17, 24

McKenzie, Vashti 62

Mitchell, Ella Pearson 8
Moore, Rev. Mary 63
Moses, 9, 11, 67-68
Mott, Lucretia Collins 31

Ryan, Sarah 20
Ruether, Rosemary R. 17

Palmer, Phoebe 23, 36-37

Schori, Katherine Jefferts 65
Sisera, 9, 68
Shelton, Sarah Jackson 63
Smith, Amanda Berry 16, 21
Stanton, Alysa 65
Stanton, Elizabeth Cady 31

Taylor, Barbara Brown 14-15
Trimm, Trudie 54
Truth, Sojourner 16
Tubman, Harriet 41
Tyler, Rev. Carolyn 61

U.S. Women's Rights Movement 1848 16

Wesley, John 20-21, 23
Willard, Emma Hart 16-18
Wollstonecraft, Mary 16

ABOUT THE AUTHOR

The late **Rev. Dr. Louis Blake Hathorn**, a native of Noxapater, Mississippi, a former educator, and community leader, was an award-winning author; his textbook *Social Justice and Christianity* covers 500 years of Christian social reform and resistance. He was the Sheppard of **Sweet Home M.B. Church** in Lexington, Mississippi for over four decades. He was also the pastor of **Mt. Sinai M.B. Church** in Louisville, Mississippi.

DEDICATION

This book is dedicated to all the women preaching God's 'good news' to God's children around the world. God speed to you. Keep the faith!

AUTHOR'S NOTE:

John Wesley ordained the first female Methodist preacher in 1784 - 232 years ago. At that time, women were restricted to the kitchen. They couldn't own property, vote, or preach; in fact, a woman could be whipped in her house by her husband like a child.

Like most southern preachers, I possessed old views of women, and was against women preaching until I witnessed a woman preacher move the congregation to its feet.

The crowd roared, "Woman Preach." I along with several male preachers stood with the crowd. Like me, other men must feel God's power at work to realize that God calls women to do His work.

Rev. Dr. Louis Blake Hathorn

ACKNOWLEDGEMENTS

First and foremost, I give thanks to my Father and Savior Jesus Christ who has ordered my steps and been my ever-present help.

I am also indebted to the many family, friends and parishioners that have prayed countless fervent prayers on my behalf. Special thanks goes to the members of the Sweet Home. M.B. Church of Lexington, and Mt. Sinai M.B. Church of Louisville, Mississippi for having everlasting faith in me as their pastor.

I thank my entire family: my three children, Shintri, Chellani and Blake for never giving up on me and sticking by me. A very humble and special thanks goes out to my wife, Mrs. Claranett M. Hathorn for her untiring love, concern for my wellbeing and encouragement. She has never ceased in her support and being a virtuous woman of God. It is true that a man, who findeth a wife, findeth a good thing. I have found my wife, which has proven to be the **best thing** for me.

Rev. Dr. Louis Blake Hathorn

Order Meredith Etc Titles:
www.meredithetc.com (online)

Textbooks

Social Justice and Christianity discusses social justice leaders from the Popes who blessed ships sailing to the Americas to the pastors who embraced the Fight for $15.

James Meredith: Warrior and the America that created him is a biography of James Meredith in the context of the America that created him and his generation.

Fiction

Murder mystery based on complex plots set in contemporary Memphis, TN which leads Detectives to a multi-million dollar illegal prison contraband racket, a serial killer...

Novella about a fierce family feud which lands one of its own in jail causing him to lose his voting rights, while his younger sister becomes the sole beneficiary of the family estate.

Meredith Etc a small press

Blog: meredithetc.com
facebook Meredith Etc
Meredithetc

Memoirs

Hideous family secrets, redemption, intergenerational incest, rape, murder.

Mary, born to sharecroppers, during Jim Crow, grew up and broke ground in business and music.

Teen homelessness, teen marriage, child abuse, child abandonment, deportation.

Poetry

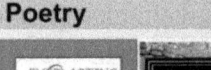

Tragedy, Yet, Triumphant

Social Justice & Christianity

www.meredithetc.com - *where you can read yourself happy!*

38 NOTES

[i] Ella P. Mitchell. (1991). *Women: To preach or not to preach.* Valley, PA: Judson Press, 19.

[ii] Ella P. Mitchell, Ibid, 19.

[iii] Ella P. Mitchell, Ibid, 1.

[iv] Rosemary R. Ruether. (2005, September). Women ascend the pulpit. *USA Today,* 66.

[v] Newsweek. (April, 2010). History of women in Catholicism. 155 (*15*), 2.

[vi] Sohani Crockett. (June, 2006). It's a woman's job now. *U.S. Catholic,* 31.

[vii] Neela Banerjee. Clergywomen find hard path to pulpit. *New York Times,* (26 August 2006), 1A.

[viii] Jennifer W. Tait. (April, 2004). "I Received my Commission from Him, Brother." *Christian History & Biography,* 82, 36.

[ix] Lucy Lind Hogan. (2000). Negotiating personhood, womanhood, and spiritual equality: Phoebe Palmer's defense of the preaching women, *ATQ,* 216.

[x] Jennifer W. Tait. (April, 2004). "I Received my Commission from Him, Brother." *Christian History & Biography,* 82, 36.

[xi] Jennifer W. Tait. 38.

[xii] Ella P. Mitchell, Ibid, 19.

[xiii] William D. Booth. (2001). The open door for women preachers: Acts 2:17, 18; 21:9; Romans 10:15; Ephesians 4:11. *The Journal of Religious Thought, Pastor's Corner,* 108.

[xiv] William D. Booth. 115

[xv] Lucy Lind Hogan. 214.

[xvi] Beverly A. Zink-Sawyer. (2000). From preachers to suffragists: Enlisting the pulpit in the early Movement for Woman's Rights. *Union Theological Seminary and the Presbyterian School of Christian Education,* 197.

[xvii] Ella P. Mitchell, Ibid, 176.

[xviii] Ella P. Mitchell, Ibid, 117.

[xix] Ella P. Mitchell, Ibid, 116.

[xx] Anne Wortham. (2000). Sojourner Truth. *World & I,* 15 (*3*), 17.

[xxi] Anne Wortham. (2000). Sojourner Truth. *World & I,* 15 (*3*), 17.

[xxii] Van Biema & David Kauffman et al. Rising above the stained-glass ceiling. *Time,* June 2004, 163 (*26*), 2.

[xxiii] Alan Bunce. Diversity makes its way to the pulpit. *Christian Science Monitor,* 88(*219*), 2.

[xxiv] Paul Sullins. (2000). The Stained Glass Ceiling: Career Attainment for Women Clergy. 61 (*3*), 244.

[xxv] Paul Sullins. 244.

[xxvi] Judith L. Weidman. (1981). Women Ministers: How women are redefining traditional roles. New York, NY: Harper & Row, 3.

[xxvii] Randy J. Sparks. (2001). Religion in Mississippi. *United States of America: Mississippi Historical Society,* 259.

[xxviii] Randy J. Sparks. Ibid, 259.

[xxix] Keri Wyatt Kent. (2008). A Reverent Maverick. *Christianity Today*, 49.

[xxxi] U.S. Catholic. *Preacher Women.* May 23, 2007, 72 (7), 32.
[xxxii] U.S. Catholic. 35.
[xxxiii] Lynn Norment. (June, 2004). In the male domain of pasturing: Women find success in the pulpit. *Ebony*, November 1981, 101.
[xxxiv] Neela Banerjee. Clergywomen find hard path to pulpit. *New York Times*, (26 August 2006), 1A.
[xxxv] Van Biema & David Kauffman, et al. Rising above the stained-glass ceiling. *Time*, June 2004, 163 (*26*), 3.
[xxxvi] Charlie Lee-Potter. It's a women's job now. *New Statesman*, 30.
[xxxvii] Melody K. Hoffman. (July, 2009). 1st Black woman Rabbi's Journey to history, *Jet*, 18.
[xxxviii] Mark J. McGrath. (June, 1993). Buried treasures: Rediscovering women's roles in the bible. *U.S. Catholic*, 58 (6), 13.

www.ingramcontent.com/pod-product-compliance
Lightning Source LLC
Chambersburg PA
CBHW060849050426
42453CB00008B/921